SCOTT ALEXANDER KING

ANIMAL
DREAMING

ORACLE CARDS

ANIMAL DREAMING
ORACLE CARDS

Published by Blue Angel Publishing®
80 Glen Tower Drive, Glen Waverley,
Victoria, Australia 3150
Phone: +61 3 9574 7776
Fax: +61 3 9574 7772
E-mail: info@blueangelonline.com
Website: www.blueangelonline.com

Illustrations by Karen Branchflower
E-mail: info@animaldreaming.com

Design © 2007 Blue Angel Publishing
Edited by Tanya Graham

Blue Angel is a registered trademark of Blue Angel Gallery Pty. Ltd.

ISBN: 978-0-9802865-3-3

For Patrick

"... Ask now the Beasts
And they shall teach thee;
And the Fowls of the air,
And they shall teach thee;
Or speak to the Earth,
And it shall teach thee."

Job 12: 7- 8

CONTENTS

CARD INTERPRETATIONS

AIR CARDS

FIRE CARDS

WATER CARDS

EARTH CARDS

Preface

~~~~~~~~~~~

The understanding that animals can be spiritually called upon to assist us in almost every aspect of our lives is a realisation that opens a floodgate of knowledge and power to those who seek their guidance. Ancient teachings suggest that we are capable of communing with the forces of nature and speaking readily to the animals. If we listen carefully to what they have to say and take the time to learn their symbolic language, the teachings say that we will be shown how to live interconnected, whole and abundant lives. The animals each have a lesson to share and we can make it our mission to learn each one and use the knowledge gained to manifest the animals' qualities and sacred wisdom into our own lives.

By invoking the power of an animal, we are seeking complete harmonious union with the strength of that animal's being. We are asking the animal to share its secrets, its Dreaming, the key to what makes it unique and in doing so we are making it vulnerable to attack. It is for this reason, as with any animal encounter, that the approach is made with humility, respect and true intent. Quietening the mind, letting go of inner tension and listening with an intuitive ear will ultimately lead to the extraordinary being found in the silence. The Sacred Silence was, and still is, the key to the receiving of Spirit and its messages. The knowledge the animals can impart is a Pathway to Power - a pathway that must be trodden with awe and respect. The power lies in the understanding of our role in life; in the honouring of the Earth as our mother, and the recognition of every living thing as our brother or sister and teacher. We must maintain a reverent attitude to all things of nature and treat everything as our equal and, in doing so, we will realise our sacred place in the Web of Life.

Introduction

Energy exists within all things of nature and can be accessed and incorporated into our own lives. The energy can be transmuted into knowledge and shared amongst the people. It is possible to translate this energy, as one would a new or foreign language, so that the wisdom may be understood and integrated into the conscious world. This information is available to everyone, so long as one's approach is executed with a deep respect and humbleness radiated from the heart, as a way of demonstrating to Spirit one's pure intent and purpose.

In ancient times it was common for an individual to seek out the advice of an Elder or respected person within the community who had fine-tuned their abilities to commune with the energies of nature. This wise person was seen as a direct link between the people and Spirit and their words were held in high esteem, for theirs were believed to have come directly from the Creator and the ancestors of the people.

Often, in order to channel the wisdom accurately or to focus the attention of the seeker, aspects of nature would be taken up and used as divinatory implements. Perhaps the wise one would look to the clouds, or the shapes forming in the smoke as it billowed from the fire. Perhaps the animals would be consulted, depending on what appeared as the seeker approached the elder. Sometimes the winds may have blown a certain way, offering inaudible wisdom with their breath. Perhaps a bag containing claws, teeth, whiskers and bones of sacred animals would be given a quick shake and upturned, with the contents spilling haphazardly onto the ground.

Depending on where and how they fell and the patterns formed as they tumbled, the wise person would have gained information relevant to the seeker, while simultaneously incorporating the Dreaming of the animals represented by the claws and teeth.

The Animal Dreaming Cards embrace this concept by figuratively taking up those claws and teeth, and in a manner more befitting our times, presenting them to the people. Instead of representing the animals in such a blatant manner, however, the cards offer beautifully illustrated portraits, with each animal's Dreaming clearly interpreted in this guidebook.

Reading the Cards

The Animal Dreaming cards have been developed with the energies of the four directions in mind, with the traditional correspondences exclusive to each direction determining the animals and the wisdom they impart.

With the Eagle delegated as card number zero, representational of 'Spirit', the first eleven cards symbolise the lessons of the East, collectively embracing the gifts of intuition, clarity of mind and illumination. The East is governed by the element 'Air', and is the birthplace of the sun each day. It is that point in time where we enter the world as a newborn child and the phase that allows us to trust our gut knowing on things.

The next eleven cards harness the energies of the North and the element 'Fire'. The animals represented by these cards co-operatively set about acknowledging the lessons of power, passion and innocence. The energy of the North symbolises the sun as it sits directly overhead at midday. It represents the teenage years when we know everything, yet nothing, at the same time. It is the phase that suggests that if we follow our true-life path we would have the potential to live a prosperous, happy and complete life.

The next eleven cards, charged with the energies of the West and the element of 'Water', embrace the emotions and the lessons of introspection, contemplation and meditation. Exemplifying the energies at dusk, the West symbolically represents the phase in life where we find ourselves asking, 'is this it?' and the choices that present themselves as a result.

The final eleven cards harness the power of midnight, the 'Earth' element and the gifts of maturity and wisdom. The animals that harness the energies of the South reveal how far we have come and the experience and acumen we have gathered along the way. It is the phase that suggests we may have achieved all that we could under the circumstances, to the very best of our abilities.

Some say that there are five elements, with the fifth signifying either Spirit or Love. The energy and the intent imbued within the forty-five Animal Dreaming cards views the fifth element as being the love and protection sought by those who walk their talk and strive to embrace a spiritual existence. The purpose of the Animal Dreaming Cards is to assist people in their healing, in their own personal connection to Spirit and in knowing and fulfilling their true purpose. This appreciation, as a portrayal of the fifth element, is imbued throughout the cards as a common perception, and must be sought out individually in a manner personal to the seeker.

Affirmation

The Animal Dreaming cards can be selected individually on a daily basis as points of focus for meditation, affirmation or daily life lessons and can be incorporated into how one approaches the world, runs one's life or interacts with other people. Such a method honours the animals in their traditional role as teachers and guides, and as a sacred link to Spirit. By consulting a different card each day we are effectively taking a Walkabout without having to leave the room. We are taking our intent and offering it to Creation by asking Spirit to send us the most appropriate sign or message to assist us with the day's events.

The Walkabout

The Walkabout was never a casual stroll taken in nature. It was a journey of Spirit, undertaken with the intention of communing with the Ancestral Spirits. A majority of the ancient cultures looked to the Earth Mother for her knowledge in this way, looking to the animals, the plants and stones, the sky, the mountains, the streams and the soil for their wisdom and guidance in times of need. The Walkabout was a way of ceasing the inner chatter. The Walk was undertaken with the intent of finding and honouring the silence within so that one may hear the quiet whispers of one's Spirit Brothers and Sisters and see with the inner eyes the wisdom of the Earth Mother. It was a way of focusing one's intent and a way of reconnecting to the web of life that interlaces everything in nature as one, originating from the same source. If we were to take a Walkabout, for example, the Dreaming of the animal or bird that first presented itself triggering feelings of reverence could be considered a harbinger of a sign or message, and interpreted as such.

Instead of taking the Walk, the cards offer the chance to receive the same sign or message in the comfort of our own home. Choosing a card embraces the entire process without expecting one to physically walk anywhere. Sitting still with the cards so that one may find the silence within before choosing a card is essential, as it creates a safe place and a sacred connection between you and the energies of Nature represented by the cards.

Alternatively, it is quite acceptable to intuitively create a spread for oneself that captures the essence of what one needs from the cards, or to adapt the cards to a traditional spread. The 'three card spread' is a generic option that essentially looks at the cards as representing past influences, the present, and future potentials that may help clarify one's life path. The Celtic Cross Spread, a common spread used in other systems, may also be adopted or adapted as a possible alternative.

Keep in mind, though, that the Animal Dreaming cards have been developed to be used in spreads designed especially for their purpose.

Interpreting the Cards

No matter what spread is decided upon, the interpretations of the cards have been intentionally written to focus only on the positive application. It is intended that should a card appear in a contrary or inverted position, the reader should simply turn the card to its upright position. This has been done with the belief that if the reader's life was free of obstacles and concerns, there should be no need to consult the cards in the first place. To consult the cards indicates a need for clarity, guidance and confirmation. To offer a negative viewpoint is to focus on fear. It threatens to deliver the reader into a place that reinforces low self-esteem and a lack of confidence. It may also negate any feelings of blossoming motivation and optimism. Most people are willing to strive for more, to achieve and to initiate healing when their lessons are approached from a perspective that suggests the glass is half full rather than half empty.

The Animal Dreaming Spreads

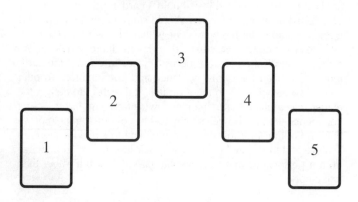

The Power Animal Spread

Power Animals are those revered as 'creature teachers'; their symbolic power relevant to the ancient beliefs and physical geography of the tribal people who traditionally shared their land. They were often celebrated as Ancestor Spirits or teachers charged with great spiritual power, each imbued with lessons and wisdom that, if acknowledged, held the power to heal, nurture and protect the people.

Card number one: The card in this position offers trust in your inherent knowing without the need for external confirmation. The animal depicted on this card banishes fear, confusion, darkness and despair. It heralds a time of courage, strength of mind, clarity and trust in your intuition.

Card number two: This animal returns us to that moment in life when we first experienced true wisdom, clarity and passion; the time when we believed we knew everything and viewed the world from a place of complete trust and expectation. This animal demonstrates how to best reclaim this sacred time of power.

Card number three: This animal invites us to journey within, to know our own spirit and to trust our own judgement. This animal guides us to a place of self-trust, self-reliance and self-acceptance.

Card number four: This animal demonstrates the lessons that we have successfully mastered or those that we might want to explore deeper to complete our understanding of who we are and what we are to become.

Card number five: This animal demonstrates how you may develop the skills needed to lead your people to a place of greatness; how you can inspire others to strive for greatness, deepen their connection to the Ancestors and heal their past and their families. This animal will help you take responsibility for your own life, your role in the world and your duty as a teacher and wise one. It offers maturity and wisdom and a medicine that comes from a very deep place.

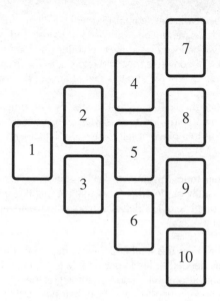

The Totem Spread

The word 'totem' literally translates to 'friend'. Totems can be employed as a means of finding out who we are, who we were and what we can become. They can help us determine what our purpose is and how we can use this knowledge to help others. Totems guide us along the pathways of life and help us to choose wisely the directions we take and the things we welcome into our personal space. Their powers are reflected through our attitudes and behaviour.

Card number one: This animal represents your true inner self and it is where you store your hopes and fears, your plans, secrets and fantasies. This animal may offer personal contests and powerful spiritual investigations that will help you step out of the shadows.

Card number two: This animal represents your innate yin (feminine / intuitive / creative) aspect.

Card number three: This animal represents your yang (masculine / tangible / conscious) aspect.

Card number four: This animal governs your personal connection to Spirit and your best line of communication with Great Mystery. This animal can be called upon to protect you as you sleep, meditate and commune with Spirit.

Card number five: This animal demonstrates how you interact with others and how they perceive you. It represents the work you do and the way in which you do it. It can even determine the direction you may want to consider to lift you out of the mundane into a place of spiritual enlightenment and purpose.

Card number six: This animal stores your memories, subconscious blockages and emotional burdens. It affords you greater understanding of the forgotten origins of your pains, fears and insecurities.

Card number seven: This animal heralded your birth and was your guardian and guide throughout your childhood. It can be called upon to initiate new beginnings.

Card number eight: This animal was your guardian and guide during the teenage years. This animal inspires you to strive, achieve and to dare. It supports the energy of the animal in position seven by grounding the innocence and offering a foundation on which new ventures may be initiated.

Card number nine: This animal often supports the transition from young adult to parent. The animal depicted on this card offers strength to those who are questioning the meaning of life. This animal is the guardian to the inner self. It acts as a mentor, a guide, a beacon of hope and, if allowed, can show you how to master the art of contemplation.

Card number ten: This animal represents you as the elder, wise one and teacher. This animal reminds you when to speak and when to observe. It embodies the level of maturity, innate wisdom and strength that comes with experience. The animal in this position echoes your integrity, your fidelity and your level of impeccability. This animal is the most sacred. It will guide you back to Spirit at the end of your Earth Walk and will be there to witness the weighing of your heart against the Feather of Truth.

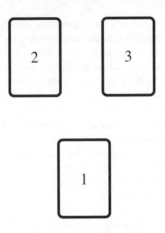

The Mother Earth, Grandmother Moon and Grandfather Sun Spread

The Earth Mother, as our true Mother, wants us to remember our Spirit; that we are not apart from the world in which we live, but rather a sacred thread in the universal tapestry. She reminds us that if we were left out or ignored, the integrity of the universal tapestry would be breached, thus weakening the potential of the Web of Life itself. The sun is a symbol of life, beauty and all that is masculine. Some say that the light of the sun represents the life-giving seed sent to Mother Earth at the beginning of time, to nurture her children and impregnate the planet and all who dwell on her with potential. The moon is the protector of humanity and the guardian of the Earth Mother. She holds all the mysteries of Creation and, when represented by the Goddess in her many forms, represents all that is feminine.

Card number one: This animal represents your connection to the Earth Mother. It reminds you to honour every living thing as your brother or sister. Everything of nature has a lesson to share and wisdom to impart. This card offers insight into how to access this knowledge, how to deepen your connection with the Earth and how to best honour Spirit's ways.

Card number two: This animal demonstrates how to honour the primary feminine influences in your life – the mothers, grandmothers, sisters, wives and daughters. This card asks you to look at the interaction you have with the women in your life and to look to the animal depicted to help deepen, heal or initiate a more meaningful relationship with one or all of them.

Card number three: This animal demonstrates how to honour the primary masculine influences in your life – the fathers, grandfathers, brothers, husbands and sons. This card asks you to look at the interaction you have with the men in your life and to look to the animal depicted to help deepen, heal or initiate a more meaningful relationship with one or all of them.

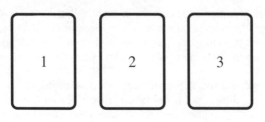

The Clarity Spread

The Clarity Spread is a quick, easy method for determining the energies moving through your life at any one given time. It offers insight into your past experiences, your present circumstances and your future potential. It helps us remove blocks (typically rooted in past experience) that prevent future movement and growth by helping us to stand purposefully in the now. By addressing the past and integrating the lessons offered by these experiences into the present, we are generally assured a positive future free of obstacles and limitation. The Clarity Spread is essentially a Stepping Stone to Power – one that affords potential healing and clarification on all levels.

Card number one: Represents your past and the opportunities your experiences are offering you to grow and prosper. The animal depicted on this card clarifies the lessons from the past you would be wise to acknowledge and integrate into your present by answering the why, how and what type questions haunting your mind, thus turning latent negative past experiences into enlightening Gifts of Power.

Card number two: Represents your present and the beauty that surrounds you at this time. This animal helps you realise the abundance already present in your life by highlighting talents, loves and other gifts from Spirit currently enhancing your life. It anchors the lessons gleaned from the past (card number one) so that you may fully integrate the acumen obtained into your life today.

Card number three: Represents a prospective abundant future and the energies best suited to help you realise it. The animal illustrated on this card is imbued with the wisdom and strength needed to help you break through familiar (and limiting) behaviour and attitudes, to see them for what they are (based on the lessons recognised with cards numbered one and two) and to abandon them in favour of a more productive, more personally relevant set of values and beliefs.

INTERPRETING

THE CARDS:

Air

0.
EAGLE – Spirit

Zero rests at the very core of our numerical system - suspended somewhere between the positive and negative. While suspended in the womb, we sit at the heart of our own personal universe; barren like the number zero with seemingly nothing physical to offer, but innately imbued with a desire to go forth and learn. We sit as if perched on a precipice, waiting for the best opportunity to take the leap of faith that will initiate the rest of our lives.

The concept of Spirit is very much like the number zero. Spirit sits between the worlds – it is neither here nor there. Spirit may be intangible but it is not inaccessible. People often say that they cannot believe in something they cannot see. Air is not visible to the naked eye but we trust that it is there. We experience it every time we inhale, when a baby takes its first breath and every time we see a flower swaying in a breeze. We have no tangible proof of its existence, but based on trust and experience we have faith in the fact that it will always be there. The concept of Spirit is exactly the same. We have to trust that it is there and that when we are in need, our calls will be heard.

The Eagle is revered as a symbol of the Creator Spirit because of its ability to soar to breath-taking heights. Its piercing eyesight is said to bare witness to the fears we keep locked deep within our consciousness; our vulnerabilities, discomforts and inabilities. And it has the sacred capacity to know our heart of hearts, our sincere and purest intent, and our true essence.

If Eagle has soared into your cards today, be comforted in the knowledge that Spirit is guiding and protecting you while you make decisions and grapple with the obstacles you are inevitably going to face as you journey through life. Eagle comes as a reminder that in order to achieve anything in this life, educated leaps of faith must be taken and trust in one's inherent capabilities must be recognised and brought to the fore. Without these qualities life is full of possibility but devoid of movement or purpose.

Not until we identify our strengths and the opportunities they afford can we realise the potency and promise within our lives. Not until we find the courage to take the first step and witness the chain of events that lead to the final one can it be realised that all is as it should be.

1.
LYREBIRD ~ Genetic Memory

Lyrebird supports the concept of genetic memory through its ability to remember the forest sounds of over 200 years ago. Flawlessly mimicking repetitious sound, the older birds pass on to their young the sounds they were taught by their parents, thus literally handing-on sacred lineal knowledge to the next generation. The young instinctively learn the sounds almost as if they are hearing them through their Ancestor's ears.

Awareness of genetic memory is often confused with that gleaned from past lives. The notion of past lives advocates that we have all had life experiences in other time periods. It also lends itself to the possibility that we may have lived the lives of notable people from history.

Many speak of recalling their past lives, remembering first hand their lives as a famous person in a familiar historical setting. Accounts of children recalling life memories outside the realms of physical possibility are being documented more and more these days. Lyrebird invites us to ponder the thought that, instead of these being personal memories, might they not be the memories of our Ancestors? Experiences passed on genetically for us to access and to learn from in our current lifetime?

Within every individual cell that collectively makes us whole, reside the keys to the unlocking of the memory of past experiences passed from one generation to the next. Such memory is inherited and genetic in nature.

Genetic memory represents all that we have ever been. It embodies all that we have ever experienced, all that we have ever encountered and all that we have ever understood. It represents all that our body inherently recognises without explanation; knowledge that cannot be justified or rationalised. It is a fair argument, therefore, that our body remembers the memories of everything ever witnessed by us since the beginning of time.

If the Lyrebird has flaunted his way into your cards today, you are being primed for a time of great remembering. The Ancestors are calling to you from the Void to remember a connection shared or a lifetime had in a period long gone. Such effort will provide deeper understanding of the relationships and responsibilities you have now, enabling you to put them into context, thus affording you greater clarity and personal direction.

2.
MOUSE ~ Scrutiny

There is a fable that tells of a Mouse that once freed a Lion securely fastened by rope bindings. The Lion had initially scoffed at the Mouse's timid offer of assistance, suggesting that if a mighty and brave Lion could not break the ropes then what chance did a Mouse have of doing better? The Mouse insisted and, little by little, chewed through the knots to eventually set the Lion free.

The Mouse reminds us that if we look at life from varying vantage points, remain vigilant and take one step at a time, checking our progress regularly, we will never be hindered by trouble.

The Mouse is small and wily enough to go through life without being detected. Although he lives a life of cunning and deceit, his wisdom is offered today in the form of awareness. He teaches us to be ever alert to the tell tale signs that things are not as they should be. Mouse is mindful of never ignoring the small, seemingly insignificant details that threaten to haunt him later. He is aware that he may some day feel the searing pain of Owl's talons in his back should he become complacent and let his guard down.

Mouse uses his keen sense of smell to constantly test the air for danger. He allows his whiskers to touch everything in his path as a way of checking that all is as it should be.

If Mouse has appeared in your cards you are being encouraged to touch everything with your symbolic whiskers, particularly when signing agreements or contracts, or when considering new projects, proposals or ventures involving other parties. Mouse reminds us to remain vigilant to the smaller aspects first and to check for pitfalls or hidden opportunities before rushing into anything.

Mouse promises that scrutiny will ensure we never overlook the obvious. He demonstrates that even those who have very little influence in the way of the world can reach places of prominence if they hold great expectations.

Mouse reveals quite effectively that sometimes strength of mind prevails over strength of body. Answers to difficult situations often lie in how the problems are perceived.

BUTTERFLY
Transformation

3.
BUTTERFLY – Transformation

Butterfly Dreaming works vibrationally with the number three. Since ancient times three has represented creative power and growth. Three was the first number to traditionally represent the 'whole'. As a symbol, the number three contains an obvious beginning, middle and end. It is the Triad – a term which embodies the universal nature of the world as Heaven, Earth and Sea. It is life as a whole, encompassing the three phases of the moon, for example, the three phases of human development (Maiden/Youth, Mother/Father and Crone/Sage) and humanity itself, being made up of the body, mind and soul.

As the Butterfly moves from one developmental stage of life to another (as it moves from the darkness and confines of the chrysalis to the light of freedom), it shows trust in its ability to grow and adapt to new situations.

Butterfly promises that when contemplating change, and when the time is right, she will offer three potent windows of opportunity to rebirth, grow and heal on all levels – with each window augured by 'butterflies in the stomach', lasting approximately one week. Such a period is typically followed by a figurative death, represented by the ending of a job or relationship, a bout of depression, a breakdown or a sudden shift in awareness. Only after the darkness is celebrated can clarity and gratitude be reinstated.

When initiating change, wait for the 'butterflies in the stomach'. This is the best time to get things moving. However, if you feel the butterflies in the stomach, but cannot activate anything due to extenuating circumstances, do not fret. Butterfly offers three windows of opportunity. Simply wait until the next time the butterflies are felt. But be aware that if the second opportunity is left unheeded, the third chance may very well be the last one offered for some time.

To have Butterfly flit its way into your cards is to be encouraged to harness the silence so that you may better hear those around you, both corporally and ethereally; those who may be calling to you from their heart rather than with their voice.

4.
OWL ~ Deception

The Owl is a silent flyer due to the velvety surface of its feathers, making the element of surprise the strength of its assault, enhanced by the fact that the attack usually comes from a source completely unsuspected by its victim. The first that the unwary Mouse knows of the presence of an Owl is the pain of sharp talons felt in its sides.

The Dreaming lesson here is that of deception. Today, according to its pooled spiritual teachings, the Owl warns us not to assume that all is well all of the time. People and situations we trust may not be completely trustworthy, but Owl has the ability to see what others may miss. The gift of this Dreaming is to be undeceived by external appearances and to discover the truth beneath them.

A bird that chooses to hunt at night, the Owl is up until dawn. She is one of the few creatures that actually wait for the sun to come up before retiring for a well-earned rest. She literally welcomes the sun as it illuminates and warms the horizon each morning. As such, she symbolically sheds light on those areas of our life in which we are being deceived by camouflage, fraudulence, pretence or duplicity.

Owl's wisdom allows us to know when we are stuck in the content of our own lives, oblivious to the fact that we are wandering aimlessly through life. Owl sheds light on these moments, so that clarity may be retrieved and stability salvaged.

By helping us to find light at the end of an otherwise pitch-dark tunnel, Owl promises a time of approaching lucidity, new beginnings and promise.

If Owl has silently swooped into your cards today, you are being cautioned that you are perhaps being deceived by the apparently innocent motives of another. Owl's appearance may be a warning that you need to quickly ascertain the integrity hidden behind these motives and determine how they may affect or influence your view of the world.

The Owl has been gifted with clear night-vision which, when employed with the right intent, affords us the ability to see what others may miss.

5.
OYSTERCATCHER ~ Concealment

A symbol of supreme Mystery according to Christian tradition, the pearl is a metaphor for truth and wisdom.

A beautiful seabird with a powerful bill used for prying open oysters, the Oystercatcher has plumage stained with a mark that strongly resembles the sign of the crucifix. Christian tradition has it that the Oystercatcher once concealed Jesus under a mass of seaweed when it learned of the danger he was in. Out of gratitude for its selfless act of concealment, the Oystercatcher was marked thereafter with the sign of the cross to venerate its Dreaming.

So long as you are not intentionally lying to anyone, including yourself, and no harm comes to anyone, including yourself, all is as it should be. Oystercatcher is not a supporter of the conceal-ment of truth as a means of controlling others, but rather as a way of protecting one's sense of security and self-esteem. Choosing not to reveal a truth is not necessarily lying. If the topic never arises, one does not have to speak of it. It is no one's business but your own, so long as it does not interfere with or damage another's view of the world.

If you look at your life and realise that a portion of yourself is being repressed for reasons that no longer serve you, turn this aggravating grit of sand into something precious. Open up and reveal it as your Pearl of Wisdom – the aspect of your self that you yearn to have seen as sacred and worthy of public scrutiny.

If the Oystercatcher has flown into your cards today, ask what side of yourself you are concealing from the world, either intention-ally or inadvertently. What aspects are you attempting to hide from yourself? What facets of your life would you like to see revealed and honoured by all?

You are being reminded that there is a time and a place for every-thing, and that if it seems appropriate to conceal the truth of who or what you are, then do it, but if it now seems inappropriate, then stop.

6.
DRAGONFLY ~ Illusion

Like the Butterfly, Dragonfly embodies the regenerative powers of rebirth.

After mating, Dragonflies deposit their eggs in water, where they hatch and develop into ferocious aquatic larvae before transmuting into adult Dragonflies. The Dragonfly emerges from a fully aquatic lifestyle to a creature capable of full aerial flight, no longer restricted to the confines of the pond or river into which it initially hatched.

Dragonfly experiences a symbolic death at the midpoint of its life. After a period of obligatory dormancy, the Dragonfly re-emerges as an apparently completely new creature, with deceptively iridescent wings that seem to glisten with the changing light – a transformation Dragonfly is yearning to see you make today.

As children we may be taught values and beliefs that are based on cultural or family tradition and morals that may be simply regarded as outdated in today's society. These illusions seem so real, though, that we accept them as our reality.

As we mature, these ways often contradict our self-discovered principles and we learn to adapt them accordingly. However, depending on how deeply these beliefs are ingrained, sometimes we cannot shake them in order to make way for our own. When this happens we find ourselves in turmoil because we feel as though we are dishonouring our culture or family by trying to follow our own truth.

If Dragonfly has darted into your cards today, you are being urged to break through self-endorsed limitations that hinder your development and growth. Look at yourself and acknowledge the illusions you may have woven around yourself as a form of protection. Ask yourself if these illusions were put in place to prevent you from seeing a truth or to prevent others from seeing the real you. Have you started believing in your own deception, in a falsity created originally to protect your sense of security or self-esteem?

Your view of the world may be restricted by your tainted perception of what is real and what is not and as a result, the view the rest of the world has of you may also be unfairly tainted.

7.
BILBY - Fear

Vulnerability is a keynote of the Bilby, whose numbers have dropped so dramatically that it now sits on the verge of extinction. Fear surrounds this unassuming marsupial and is demonstrated both through the animal's nervy disposition and the concerns wild-life authorities hold for its survival in the wild.

The problem with fear though, is that it grows like wildfire. The moment fear is welcomed into your thinking it bursts into life and quickly dominates any situation. If not properly managed and treated it will manipulate and envelop your very soul, eventually crippling your ability to see clearly and to operate effectively.

Most of us journey through life working largely from two basic lesson manuals labelled clearly with the words 'Love' and 'Fear'. Whenever we are faced with a choice or a dilemma we check these manuals. Most people favour one over the other, checking the pages for answers and seeking confirmation that is usually based on previous experience.

If the Bilby has appeared in your cards, be brave enough to ask yourself which book you think you favour. Be honest. Like most people, you may be surprised to find yourself thumbing through a well-worn 'Book of Fear'. Don't dismay, though - Bilby is offering to symbolically listen for, harness and carry the burdens of your fears for you at this time. But this will only be a temporary arrangement. It is vitally important that you realise where your fears lie, and for you to develop your own strategies to reverse their influence within your life.

Look to the Bilby and allow him to teach you how to control your fears so that they do not envelop your soul and prevent you from realising your true destiny.

Bilby offers a warning that the more we focus on our fears the more we will ultimately attract them. Bilby teaches how to reject fear, and how to alternatively use that energy to manifest abundance, love and good health within our lives.

8.
BROLGA ~ Dance

Spontaneous movement, inspired by a steady rhythmic sound and a receptive atmosphere, is an ancient yet simple way of opening oneself up to the productive cycles of Mother Earth and the nurturing energies of the Universe.

The Brolga, as a solar influenced creature, was traditionally viewed as a symbol of power and righteousness and the bringer of sacred dance. It could be assumed that Brolgas incorporate movement and dance into their mating rituals in the belief that if they dedicate themselves to Spirit and express who they are through dance, their mate will not only see their physical form, but also their heart of hearts and their worthiness as a mate and life partner.

Many of us are told at an early age that we cannot dance and that we have no rhythm. As we grow we become afraid to express our true selves and so we only dance in the privacy of our own homes for fear of being ridiculed. This is just one way in which we as individuals become fragmented from who we truly are.

If Brolga has danced into your cards today, you are being shown that dance can be your bridge into other worlds. You are being reminded that sacred dance holds the potential to reconnect you to the Source and the sacredness being nurtured within your consciousness. Through dance, you can experience the very unity of the Universe.

When you feel pressured, no matter where you are, close your eyes and breathe, allowing your body to reconnect to the rhythm of the Earth Mother's heartbeat and the music orchestrated by the sounds of Nature. Find the stillness and participate in the sacred dance of Creation on a level that does not interfere with your daily routine. Simply still your mind and celebrate the inner dance – the freedom of movement that comes with 'just being'. Feel the presence of Spirit. Feel the peace that comes with the wisdom and the ancient knowledge found within the internal dance as it permeates your body. This is your dance that connects you to the Ancients and the Ancestor Spirits of the land.

Let Brolga show you how to tap into its power and allow it to shift you from the mundane to the extraordinary within your own life.

9.
BAT ~ Rebirth

Just as a baby rests inverted in the womb waiting for its moment of birth, the Bat hangs upturned in the cave waiting for night to fall; the cave an ancient analogy for the Womb of Mother Earth.

As the Bat exits the cave, it symbolically recreates the act of birth as well as demonstrating our desire to step out of the darkness of uncertainty and to symbolically rebirth ourselves.

The image of the Bat flying out of its cave denotes desire for new beginnings or the chance to start from scratch in one or more areas of our life. It alludes to the idea of completely rebirthing who and what we are, as if re-emerging from our mother's womb as a new being. Rebirth signifies shedding all the outworn aspects of our life. It represents a complete reshuffle of how we view the world and how we see ourselves within it. It embraces the complete letting go of our very nature so that we may rebuild it, brick by brick, to reveal the true essence of who we were meant to be.

Although rebirth is generally seen as a symbolic process, renewal of one's energies can be achieved on many levels – emotional, physical and spiritual.

Bat heralds a time of discarding old practices and of adopting opinions that nurture rebirth, symbolised by stepping into a new phase or facet of life.

To resist one's fate, or to push against the tide and to deny the inevitability of such an important transformation, usually results in the prolonging of our suffering. It is our destiny to grow and become our future. It is Spirit's will … but in order to do so we must be prepared to face a symbolic time of death, and welcome a time of rebirth.

If Bat has flown into your cards today, be prepared to consciously face all your emotional issues and to remove the obstacles that are preventing your life from flowing smoothly. You must be prepared to cut out any dead wood and to remove the garbage if you are ever to encourage new growth.

10.
COCKATOO ~ Illumination

Some say that in the beginning there was perpetual darkness - a gentle Void, a blanket of nothingness that tenderly swathed the universal plains.

Within this fertile emptiness the Great Mother stirred, as if waking from eternal slumber. As though trying to recall some distant memory she began to unfold, twisting and churning, dreaming her self into fruition. She began to reach out into the darkness as a massive expanse of nurturing energy that seduced everything it encountered, willingly drawing all into her protective Womb.

Sulphur-crested Cockatoo's dark sister, the Black Cockatoo carries the Genetic Memory of this sacred time and, within her Dreaming, helps us to take control of our life by insisting that we grow at our own pace and learn what we need to know in our own time.

She encourages us to just sit in contemplation and wait for the mysteries of our life to unfold without consciously seeking answers. At the appropriate time, when our mind is still and our heart is at ease, Black Cockatoo passes the torch of illumination to her sister, the Sulphur-crested Cockatoo.

To have Sulphur-crested Cockatoo appear in your cards is an indication that you are being primed for clarity to dawn in relation to one or more aspects of your life, and for stability to once again reign supreme.

Sulphur-crested Cockatoo offers a time of illumination when truths will be revealed, when energy will flow more easily and obstacles will begin to dissipate.

As a guardian of the East Gate and an emissary of the sun, the Sulphur-crested Cockatoo promises a time of mental clarity, clear vision, enhanced intuition and stability.

11.
HAWK ~ Messages

The Hawk is said to be one of the Great Solar Birds that are able to stare directly at the sun without having to squint their eyes to lessen the glare.

To be able to look directly into the sun and not have to look away is symbolic of being able to look directly at an issue and to see what needs to be acknowledged and addressed, for the self and others.

To witness a Hawk in flight, to hear its cry, or to find one of its feathers suggests you are about to receive a sign or a gift from Spirit. Hawk's cry may indicate a bountiful harvest or an impending time of abundance, while the finding of a feather sometimes portends the birth of a child or a spiritual gift about to awaken within the receiver.

If Hawk has appeared in your cards today you are being put on alert for signs that may fruitfully guide you to the next phase of your life. You are being asked to remain vigilant and willing to act at a moment's notice.

You are also being told that it is okay to ask for signs indicating when messages are about to come so that you do not miss them. For example, asking Spirit through meditation or prayer that the messages be pre-signed by the appearance of, for example, a woman wearing predominantly yellow who will ask to take your photograph, is an obvious and precise way of knowing exactly when to be at your most attentive. Ask that the Spirit of the Hawk carry this request to Spirit with the clear understanding that as soon as a woman presents herself, dressed predominantly in yellow and asks to take your photo, Spirit will send an obvious message, sign or omen that will help you to see your future clearly; free of the usual emotional blockages or physical obstacles that have hindered your path in the past. The woman will act as your trigger; your signpost that tells you when to stop and listen for Spirit's guidance.

INTERPRETING

THE CARDS:

Fire

12.
EMU ~ Endurance

A solar influenced creature, Emu speaks of the responsibility afforded to fathers who find themselves raising their children single-handedly. Emu Dreaming lends itself to the teaching of effective parenting skills and the endurance that is required to execute the role, especially under difficult conditions.

The Emu, being a grounded, flightless bird, offers real and practical relief to the single father. As a 'yang' totem, Emu demonstrates the practical skills needed to guide and raise a child when the nurturing and protective energies of the mother are absent. Emu offers the resilience needed to cope with the day-to-day tasks that tire and exhaust, especially when a job or career is extra-curricular to the responsibilities of the lone parenting role.

Alternatively, the Emu can also assist the single mother by offering the masculine support lacking due to the absent father, so that her energies may be preserved and rejuvenated. By invoking the support of the male Emu's Spirit, the children will sense the presence of male energy, pressure will be alleviated for the mother, and stamina sustained. Assuming that the Emu energy is being radiated through the heart of the mother or the residual energy of their absent father, the children will acknowledge the harmony created within the relationship they have with their mother. Emu Dreaming subsequently renders the mother's role more grounded, balanced and less emotional, particularly if the role of single mother is new.

If Emu has strolled into your cards today, look at how you are holding up physically and emotionally to the stresses of life. Perhaps you need to pace yourself better so that you are able to maintain a manageable level of endurance.

Emu promotes a holistic approach to life that incorporates a healthy mind/healthy body philosophy while encouraging you to seize personal quiet time for replenishment whenever you are able.

Emu demonstrates how to integrate the positive and supportive aspects of both our 'yin' and 'yang' aspects by drawing their wisdom into everything we do, thus enriching our view of the world and our place (and that of our children) within it.

13.
CUSCUS ~ Calmness

Classified as one of the seven principal sins (according to Christian belief), 'sloth' denotes opposition to labour or physical exertion of any sort. Some see it as being nothing more than a lack of caring. In everyday terms, the description may be attributed to those within the community who decide not to participate in making society a better place for all, exhibiting the attitude of 'why should I?' followed by the comment, 'they have never done anything for me'. They fail to see any advantage in trying, instead opting to divert their energy into other things.

Unlike the South American Sloth, whose Dreaming is superficially described above, Cuscus imparts a sense of calm rather than lethargy. It endorses approaching life at a pace that suits and not rushing unnecessarily into making decisions that could later seem rash.

Cuscus says that to take slow, purposeful steps is a sure-fire way of ensuring a long, safe, bountiful trip. He advocates embarking optimistically on life's journey with a clear view of your destination.

It is the way of Cuscus to tackle all tasks with a sense of calmness, even if it takes all day. To do something constructive, even though it may take a while, is far better than doing nothing, or worse still, expecting someone else to do it for you; a tactic endorsed by the lazy Sloth.

Cuscus rejects idleness and believes that everything in life is worth considering – and if it is worth doing, it is worth doing well. Although Cuscus outwardly rebuffs the notion of physical exertion, he does apply solid effort when tackling new projects. Although his eagerness and enthusiasm may appear wanting to the incidental onlooker, the truth is he never jumps on board immediately or pushes anything away without first pondering the pros and cons. He takes his time and contemplates the best plan of attack. And then he commits – sooner or later. Cuscus suggests approaching all tasks little by little – like moving a mountain one grain of sand at a time. Being a Sloth gets you nowhere – fast. Putting effort into doing nothing takes just as much energy as initiating the first steps forward.

Cuscus Dreaming affirms that there is an explicit distinction between laziness and carefulness, or sloth and calmness, with neither to be mistaken for the other.

14.
SNAKE ~ Transmutation

Snake can be viewed as being both feminine and masculine in nature, both solar and lunar-influenced, an emissary of life and death, and of healing and venom. It embodies all possibilities, being masculine in form and phallic in nature, while traditionally accompanying the ancient Mother deities as symbols of intuition and wisdom. It has arbitrated the three worlds since the Dreamtime as the lightning and solar rays of the Sky Realm, the primeval waters of Mother Earth, and the Underworld in which it dwells.

The Celts saw the Snake as a powerful symbol of fertility, often depicting Serpents in their artwork with eggs lodged firmly in their mouths – emblematic depictions of Creation, with the masculine seed meeting and joining with the female egg.

While embracing the promise of new life, the Snake can be seen as representative of the healing we must accept if we intend to move into the next phase of our life in a complete and fertile way. As a symbol now employed by the medical fraternity, the Caduceus is a stylised emblem incorporating a pair of Snakes entwined together in the sacred act of copulation, working themselves as one around a staff, taking a symbolic journey to the higher, mystical realms of Before we can welcome what we yearn for into our lives, we must first be prepared to identify the things we no longer want or need.

There is no such thing as a sick person who is not grieving for something. If we are grieving for some aspect of life that we feel is out of our reach, no matter how hard we twist and turn in a vain attempt to draw it closer to us, the grief we feel will eventually make us ill.

The presentation of the Snake card is a way of gently pointing out that you need to look deep within yourself and honour those aspects that pose the threat of making you ill. We have to hand them over so that we may see clearly again, allowing us to move forward with confidence and a renewed sense of purpose. Snake encourages us to look at our baggage, our burdens and our pain and transmute them into new opportunity and new life. She offers us the chance to physically rebirth ourselves by strengthening us emotionally and deepening our relationship with Spirit.

15.
CASSOWARY – Respect

One creature or another occupies every square inch of our Earth Mother. The moment we leave our space, we step into that of another. We become their visitor, invited or not. When we drink from a stream or pick fruit from a tree, we are sharing this source of nourishment with other creatures. We share the air we breathe, the warmth of the sun, the refreshing breeze of the four winds and the rain that falls from the sky, with every other living thing on this Earth.

We have to view our life as being the only one we will ever have and honour this chance to the utmost. We have to look at every lesson that is presented as being more important than the last. We only have one Earth and it is up to us to honour the space we inhabit while we are here. Simple.

If Cassowary has swaggered into your cards today, you are being asked to address your sense of Sacred Space and the way in which you treat the Sacred Space of others. If we honour and respect our space, others will learn to respect theirs and if we honour the space of others, they will learn to respect ours.

It is okay to refuse the inappropriate or interfering ways of others. Our Sacred Space is our territory and we have the right to feel safe within it. Our home and everything associated with it; our possessions, our body, our feelings, our values and beliefs can all be viewed as Sacred Spaces, and just as a wild animal will only allow other animals who instinctively respect territorial boundaries to enter their Sacred Space, we are encouraged by the Dreaming of the Cassowary to follow suit.

It is not important what others think of you. How you view yourself is what counts. You have to live with yourself and to feel proud of how you go about doing it.

Cassowary says that in order to attract respect it is vital to radiate self-respect, to show pride in your achievements, to radiate self-worth and to adopt and mirror the favourable qualities of the people that are drawn to you, rather than focusing on their negative traits.

16.
KOOKABURRA ~ Healing

Taking responsibility for your own healing is probably one of the most confronting things anyone can do, especially if the intention is to acknowledge and release pent up pain, confusion and resentment, which are common by-products of years of postponed healing.

In our times, it is common for people to live their entire lives without ever truly healing many of their past painful experiences and long-held resentments. Most of the time these individuals do not realise there is an alternative to the internal suffering caused when we ignore the need for healing or fail to see that there is healing to be done. It is often ignorance rather than denial that prevents healing from taking place.

The Kookaburra has a distinctive call that strongly resembles human laughter, thus earning it the title of 'the Laughing Kookaburra'. Many assume therefore, that the message of the Kookaburra is that of lightening up and learning to laugh at yourself. It may be true that its laughter inspires others to laugh along with it, and this rather obvious assessment of Kookaburra's Dreaming is sometimes relevant. But the truth of the matter is that if Kookaburra does appear in your cards today, its true message goes far deeper than its superficial laughter.

Among their regular prey, Kookaburras catch Snakes by plunging down, seizing them behind the head, flying up high into the air and dropping them to their death. Snake is the harbinger of healing on all levels. Kookaburra therefore, as a bird that hunts Snakes, is telling you to take responsibility for your own healing and to stop laughing it off.

Although you may have never spoken of your desire to see your own healing fulfilled, those around you will have sensed the need. Verbalising your need for healing to these people will not only be a relief for you, it will result in a collective sigh from those around you. 'That explains so much …' will be the general consensus.

Kookaburra awakens us to our inner truth and, thus, the dawning of a new day. So remember, that to witness a silent Kookaburra is Spirit's way of restoring faith in our quest for personal healing.

17.
FROGMOUTH – Secret Keeper

The Frogmouth's tawny-grey plumage is reminiscent of the silver-grey hair of our Elders, the secrets they hold and the experience they can impart.

Elders were once revered as 'wise ones', simply because their wisdom had been accumulated over many years of life experience. They appeared to walk in beauty and in harmony with all things. They were seen as being 'content' and at peace with their lot in life. They were free of the mundane issues that hinder the progress of the everyday man. They had learned from their life experiences, integrating this accumulated wisdom into their future perception of life, thus freeing themselves of burdens and restrictions that promote anxiety, anger, guilt and resentment. Their knowledge was sought because they were believed to be able to see through the self-created illusions of fear and regret that bind us and prevent us from moving forward.

If Frogmouth has appeared in your cards, you are being encouraged to seek out the secrets being held in trust by your Elders. Approach them with respect and ask them to share their sacred knowledge. Ask questions about their history, their childhood and the way of their generation. Inquire as to what life was like for them, how they interacted with their peers and kin and the responsibilities expected of them by their seniors. Speak of chores, education and wars, of times spent at school, of love, fashion and economic flow.

Most importantly though, ask the Elders of Spirit, God, Creation and the medicine ways of all things. Seek their opinion on things of nature, for example, the cycles of life and the Universe. Ask about the things that make your heart sing, of what saddens you and what inspires you to reach higher levels of awareness. Ask until there is nothing more to ask, and then incorporate the memories and wisdom of these things into your life and share them, with the blessings of your Elders, as the sacred knowledge of your people.

BUSTARD
Confidence

18.
BUSTARD – Confidence

Spirit is all that is. It is the life force found in all things. Spirit resides in the mountains, the trees, the rivers and the clouds; the birds, the insects; the stones, the plants and the four winds. Everything of Creation is a celebration of Spirit – including you and me.

To know Spirit is to have unwavering confidence that we will be protected, nurtured and encouraged to live a prosperous life. To walk with Spirit is to know true abundance on all levels: healthy and happy children, meaningful relationships, a balanced life, a healthy body and a sound mind. When we recognise these things as being true abundance, Spirit welcomes more conventionally recognised forms of abundance to flow freely into our lives.

The Bustard exhibits a proud faith in the belief that Spirit and Mother Earth will provide all that is needed to live an honest, protected and humble life. It demonstrates how to achieve a modest yet confident air fuelled by trust, stillness and a discreet approach to life.

Bustard does not suggest we strip ourselves of all earthly possessions in order to live a good life, though. It simply warns that to favour material things and the attainment of money is no guarantee of an abundant and happy life.

Bustard wonders if you have stopped trusting your relationship with Spirit. Have you lost trust in your connection with the Earth Mother? Have you begun to see the accumulation of material things as being proof of your worthiness rather than the inherent connection you have with all things?

Bustard is encouraging you to sit motionless, silent within yourself, and ask whether or not you feel confident that your life is leading you in the direction you had hoped. Are you able to hold your head up, with your face aimed directly at Spirit, and say that your life is all that it was meant to be?

Bustard asks that you focus on the wealth and abundance that you already have in your life and give thanks for them. Surrender your fears and limitations and offer gratitude to the Earth Mother and to Spirit for your wonderful life, and feel confident that you will soon know great wealth on all levels.

19.
ANT - Strength

Ants are able to carry many times their own body weight in their jaws, a skill that makes their industrious lives so much easier. Using their powerful jaws to carry food, their young and the loose dirt they have to move when excavating their intricate tunnels, Ants work as a team, drawing on the strength that comes with pulling together.

Oversized jaws are prized not just for their threatening appearance, but also because they make formidable weapons. Efficient fighters, Ants rely on their body strength to physically overcome their opponents and their strength of mind to anticipate their every move.

As dynamic and analytical engineers, Ants know great endurance. Ants work toward all set goals from a communal perspective. In doing so, all tasks are approached and deliberated upon with a co-operative spirit, advanced upon with a common objective and undertaken as a team.

Such an approach ensures that all responsibilities are completed quickly and efficiently. They also understand the need for patience, because their diminutive stature makes the duration of projects much longer.

If Ant has scurried into your cards today, ask yourself if you are operating as a team member or as a sole agent. Are you honouring the role of your supervisor or boss? Are you considering the difficulty of their task? Are you honouring your spouse or lover? Are you pulling your weight around the home? Are you expecting others to take care of you? Are you taking care of them?

Find the strength to take responsibility for your own life. Do not expect others to sacrifice their values and beliefs to support yours. When you take responsibility for your life, you inspire others to do the same. A web is created in which everyone ultimately supports one another and assists each other in the ownership of joint responsibility.

By understanding and harnessing the power of Ant you will ultimately become the engineer of your own life. It will provide for the laying of solid life-foundations from which new opportunities will be offered and success will inevitably be realised.

20.
HORSE ~ Personal Power

When first introduced, Horse strengthened and deepened the people's view of the world. It afforded them greater understanding of the land because it allowed them to explore the horizon on a level never known before. With obvious links to movement and travel, Horse sanctioned the exploration and conquering of the physical setting, the breaking of boundaries and the expansion of territory.

In similar fashion, Horse Dreaming embraces the essence of Personal Power and what it means to spiritually journey within in search of inherent wisdom.

Personal Power represents the wealth of knowledge we may accumulate over a lifetime of experience which, when honoured, shifts us from the mundane and familiar into a world of unlimited potential.

According to tradition, a Horse stands symbolically at each of the four cardinal points on the great Wheel of Life, with the yellow Palomino protecting the East, the red Chestnut standing in the North, the black Horse guarding the West and the White or Dapple Grey representing the energies of the South. Each of the four directions offers a sacred gift of Power and a wealth of corresponding energetic wisdom.

It is up to us to go out and spiritually seek this knowledge and, once found, integrate it into our life. Metaphorically journeying to the East, for example, brings with it the gifts of illumination and introspection, while heading to the North inspires a healthy blend of innocence and passion. In the West we learn to understand the art of introspection and meditation, and in the South we are offered maturity and judgment.

If Horse has galloped into your cards today, you are being primed for a journey of great Power.

We all subconsciously know where our Personal Power lies, and as long as we instigate the search, we will ultimately find it - resulting in great rewards on all levels.

Remember: all journeys start with a simple step forward, with any forward movement nurturing growth, and growth leading to development and enrichment.

Promoting a sense of complete freedom, the appearance of Horse suggests travel of all kinds, both inner and outward; emotional, physical and spiritual.

21.
LIZARD – Daydreaming

Déjà vu occurs when we consciously 'bump into' vital details or aspects of daydreams had on earlier occasions.

When we daydream, we energetically leave the present in order to astrally 'check out' our potential future. While physically doing something routine, we find our conscious mind wandering, leaving the physical confines of our body on an astral level and exploring future aspects of our life. When our conscious mind realises that we have been daydreaming, we snap back and instantly forget what we have just experienced and the body of the daydream is expelled from our mind forever.

Daydreams are Spirit's way of allowing us to consciously explore our future while remaining bodily alert.

About a week or two after having your daydream, you will suddenly get the uncanny feeling that you have done this all before. Even though the conscious mind disagrees, the subconscious mind remembers visiting this time and space. It remembers that you placed yourself in this setting – astrally – weeks before, with the subliminal intention of remembering the fact on your bodily arrival.

The physical sensation is your wakeup call, meant to trigger a realisation that something in or around you offers a window of opportunity, that once acknowledged will initiate a great change of fortune in your life.

What you visualise in your daydreams, Spirit offers the map to find, and all that is left to do is follow the directions with intent and resolve.

If Lizard, a creature who spends her days basking in the sun and daydreaming her future into being, has visioned her way into your cards today, you are being advised to take serious note of what your dreams are trying to tell you. Keep a journal. Lizard wants you to look at your daydreams as viable messages from Spirit and veritable roadmaps to possibilities that would normally remain faceless for eternity.

Spirit gifted you with this life as a chance to make your mark on the world. Don't waste a single chance by choosing to ignore the unrealised but fertile potentials your dreams may be gathering and shaping for your future.

22.
WALLABY – Progression

After trauma, people often seek teachers and healers who claim to have the keys needed to help them regain peace and clarity. Despite leaving these sessions feeling confident and reassured, however, they often lose confidence in their own inherent ability to maintain wellness, and gradually find themselves regressing into confusion and emotional darkness. It is never their intent to slip back, but rather a force of habit.

This shadow space is familiar and feels safe, despite its negative pitfalls. They revert because they aren't born equipped with a clear understanding of how to turn darkness into light, or how to find sacredness in the horrors that haunt them; horrors that often hold within their recesses the keys to realising their Personal Power and

Purpose. When confronted, we usually grit our teeth, swallow hard and try to push through the pain in order to move forward in the hope of finding light at the end of the tunnel. When we repetitively visit our shadow space or examine past experiences, people may suggest we are dwelling in the past. And in reality, we may be. It is sometimes necessary, if we are to heal fully and honourably. We must visit our shadow space in a sacred way if we are to learn from it and, in time, rebirth ourselves from its limiting clutches.

Wallaby, because of its unusually shaped hind legs and bulky tail, cannot physically walk backwards. It rejects stagnation, therefore, and reluctant movement of any sort. Instead, it promotes progression, healing and growth - in forward leaps and bounds.

If Wallaby has hopped into your cards today, consider that you may be dwelling on some past event and using it as an excuse to linger in your shadow space. Despite good reason, you may be blaming the event for your lack of healing, growth or release of pain.

Wallaby is priming you to leap into the future without regret with a healthy respect for your grief. Wallaby helps you move forward to explore new horizons, take risks, avoid the temptation to look back with regret and never return to your comfort zone once you have left.

Wallaby takes the pains from the past, dissects them and extracts their purpose to find their reason. This reason is the vital ingredient in realising your Personal Power; the ingredient that can be shared among the people to aid in their healing.

'Onwards and upwards' is a motto that champions the advice Wallaby offers those who seek its counsel.

INTERPRETING

THE CARDS:

Water

23.
KOALA – Inner Journeys

If you come across a Koala in the wild, you will find it in one of two states – awake, feeding and tending to its young, or dozing in a foetal position, its rump securely wedged into the fork of a tree.

It is believed that the Koala slips into an altered state of awareness after ingesting the eucalyptus leaves that form the heart of its diet. Whilst in this state, it is mused that it can enter other realms of reality, or journey deep within the inner landscape. Once there, it is thought that the Koala gathers knowledge and is able to offer healing in ways not considered physically possible in the tangible world.

Koala also fosters the notion that, as spiritual beings, we inherently know the answers to all of our questions, with the knowledge we seek stored deep within our consciousness. Koala demonstrates the healing flight we must take in our personal quest for answers. It embraces the inner journey to the core of the deepest self.

To journey with the Koala is to quest for the ancient knowledge and spiritual awakening hidden within our consciousness. Koala represents a sacred journey that is unique for everyone, an expedition that supports the individual needs and requirements of all people.

If Koala has snoozed his way into your cards today, you are being assured that you inherently know the answers to your questions. Now is the time to start taking notice of your inner self, your innate connection to all the information of the Universe. Stop looking to others for corroboration, advice or wisdom. Take responsibility for your own life, your own path and your own destiny by listening to your heart of hearts.

Koala says that you must start your own journey; a quest that will unlock the answers you seek from a place hidden deep within your essence. The journey must begin today. Koala's healing journey is an experience of unimaginary proportions; a flight beyond the boundaries of the physical body.

With Koala, your potential for growth and transformation strengthens and your sense of self escalates. To fully embrace Koala Dreaming, you must first take responsibility for your own healing and trust that all will evolve as it is supposed to.

24.
PLATYPUS ~ Women's Wisdom

According to Aboriginal legend, the Platypus was birthed
from the forbidden coupling of two souls joined by unlawful union. Out of vengeance for their reprehensible behaviour, the Elders
transformed her into a Duck and him into a Water Rat. They were
then exiled indefinitely from their respective clans. She eventually
produced an egg, from which hatched a strange furry, duck-billed
creature equipped with four powerful webbed feet: the Platypus.

Those who have ever felt abandoned or rejected should seek the
wisdom of the Platypus. She was created under a blanket of dishonesty, judgment and betrayal, brought into this world as a result
of true, honest but devastating love.

No matter how old we are, we instinctively look to our parents, as our primary role models, for confirmation and guidance in all areas of our life. But what if that guidance is absent, or predisposed by traditional values or belief; values or beliefs inappropriate for today's world?

Platypus is not only committed to honouring her parent's heartfelt desire to see the people merge with peace and love in their hearts, but also to the empowerment of all women by reminding them of their worth, wisdom and their role as 'sorcerers', individuals charged with the power to create within the dark recesses of their womb. She works to free all women of guilt and oppression and to reinstate their connection to 'the source'.

If Platypus has swum into your cards today, you are being prepared to realise, understand and embrace the potency of your own intuition and higher levels of knowing.

A creature that swims with her eyes shut, Platypus listens to the heartbeat of the Earth Mother for direction. She looks to her inner yin and yang for guidance, thus finding the strength needed to make her own decisions. She honours her innate masculine and feminine qualities, knowing that she is more than capable of navigating herself through life without the support of others.

You are being urged to trust your own judgment, direction and endurance. This is the wisdom of all women - the ability to trust in their intuition and to consciously act with purpose. Women are natural dreamers, visionaries and mystics, but they must embrace their masculine aspects in order to realise the full potential of these gifts.

25.
RAVEN ~ Magick

As a messenger of the Void, Raven guides us to a place of healing, wholeness and connection to Spirit by reminding us of the sacredness of prayer.

Prayer sustains and enriches us. It is to converse with the divine energies of the Universe with the understanding that, in order to realise our wants and needs, all we need do is harness these divine energies in honour and remembrance of our innate connection to Spirit.

Magick is the ability to communicate our needs and to channel our purpose by sitting within the silence, ceasing the inner chatter and reconnecting with the Universe. It is to seek the assistance of Great

Mystery and to delve into the Void for answers – to call to Spirit and to ask for help.

Magick and prayer are similar. Prayer offers us the chance to talk to Spirit, while magick represents the results that come when we demonstrate perpetual faith in the power of prayer.

If Raven has paid you a visit from the Void today, you are being asked to honour your innate ability to create magick by participating in the sacred act of prayer. When you pray you must do so with a reverent appreciation of Spirit, in gratitude for the very life given to you at the time of your birth. Our prayers must be made in honour of the Earth Mother and in recognition of all the living creatures, and they must be made with the firm belief that all people shall someday look to Spirit and find the courage to walk as one. When you pray, you should ask for the best way to personally honour the ways of Spirit and to seek blessing for those close to your heart. When you finish, spend a little time in silence to honour the Void, for the silence is sacred and no words are necessary.

By embracing the Dreaming of Raven, you not only strengthen your line of communication with Spirit through prayer, you also better understand the deep wisdom that comes with knowing your purpose and the magick that comes with learning how to administer it.

Raven offers inner peace that will eventually lead to a deepening of your soul essence and a balancing of the self. Your self-perception will begin to strengthen when you open your heart to the wisdom of the Raven.

FAIRY PENGUIN
Willpower

26.
FAIRY PENGUIN - Willpower

In keeping with spiritual tradition, Penguins are celebrated as lucid dreamers; creatures capable of walking with clarity and intent in both the physical realm of ordinary landscape and that of the more obscure, non-ordinary reality.

The Fairy Penguin, for example, teaches us to picture in our mind's eye a desired outcome and coaches us to physically and abundantly bring it to fruition. His strong will and self-belief means he will never be restricted by limitation or inadequacy, and if we follow his lead, neither will we.

Having evolved over thousands of years to an aquatic lifestyle, Penguins lack the physical prowess to become airborne like other birds. The strong-willed Fairy Penguin, however, refuses to surrender to jealousy of his sky-roving cousins. Rather than limiting himself, he searches for alternative ways to fulfil his natural impulse to fly. Instead of taking flight like a regular bird and soaring through the clouds, Fairy Penguin takes to the white foam of Grandmother Ocean. An earth-bound bird, Fairy Penguin joyfully circles the water with the subtlety of a Swallow. Dipping and diving through the subterranean valleys, skimming the peaks of submerged mountains and flitting in and out of thick kelp forests, Fairy Penguin 'hawks' for fish in similar fashion to how a Flycatcher seizes insects while on the wing.

If Fairy Penguin has trundled into your cards today, know that you can overcome any limitation by adopting a resolute mindset.

Awaken your inherent creativity by listening intuitively to your dreams and trusting what they show you. Utilise your inner power now and believe in yourself because a time approaches that will require you to be a little more independent. Remove the blinkers, because you can achieve anything when you surrender your impediments by drawing on your willpower to find alternative ways of viewing them. Personal limitations cease being a problem when you seek constructive and achievable solutions within yourself.

It is time to stop playing the drama queen, to acknowledge the aspects of your life that are hindering your growth and to deal with them appropriately.

Penguin is telling you that it is time to harness the willpower needed to fulfil your dreams, no matter what they may be.

27.
MAGPIE ~ Balance

Magpie is the bringer of balance, the yin-yang of the bird world, an agent of awareness, the embodiment of 'the opposites that are equal' and the force that champions the attainment and correct use of esoteric knowledge.

She demonstrates that spiritual knowledge, and the power that comes with it, must be approached with a committed, objective mindset. It cannot be attained overnight, or bought with money. Information gleaned during a weekend workshop, for example, can only ever be considered a foundation on which real learning, learning that comes with experience and practice, takes place. True wisdom must be deserved. It must be gathered over a lifetime of study and embraced as a way of life. It must become a path of the heart, explored with absolute devotion.

Before questing for spiritual attainment, for example, we must first dedicate ourselves to becoming a whole person; a process that involves surrendering our familiar self to Spirit, so that our authentic self, hidden deep within, can emerge reborn. We must be prepared to face our fears and conquer them and turn our weaknesses into strengths and our darkest hours into gifts of power. In becoming a whole person we embark on an expedition to reclaim inner balance and authority and, in doing so, find ourselves stepping out of our comfort zone into the unknown.

Magpie is a doorkeeper to other realms; a guardian who lets only those willing to honour the sacred balance between the good and bad, light and dark and feminine and masculine in all things to explore her world.

If Magpie has swooped into your cards today, you are being guided to a place of awareness. You are being shown how to better understand the innate marriage between the opposites that are equal and the duality within all things. You are being primed for a deepening of purpose and a broadening of perception.

Magpie's arrival heralds an obligatory confrontation of fears, the reshuffling of thoughts, review of values and a loosening up of everything that has offered sustenance and strength up until now. It means being ready to walk a path of the heart to find a place of inner freedom: a quest for a better understanding of the poise that resides within you and everything of Nature.

28.
CROW ~ Law

As a creature of the Void, Crow is believed to exist in the past, present and future simultaneously, to embody darkness within light and light within darkness and to watch over all the worlds and dimensions from all viewpoints in chorus. She makes little distinction between right and wrong, but acknowledges the necessity for the existence of both. Without them, we wouldn't learn the lessons afforded by choice.

According to legend, when Crow appears, she is challenging our perceptions while daring us to follow her deep into the Void, into our consciousness, to strengthen our principles and our relationship with Spirit.

Crow encourages us to seek the wisdom found in the inner silence and to ponder our actions and reactions to life. We inherently know the difference between right and wrong. Crow asks us, therefore, to trust our judgment and make the most sensible decision when one is required.

Her appearance generally heralds a sudden but necessary change, a wake-up call or a lesson in self-discovery.

Crow is one of the sacred keepers of universal law and the custodian of ancient records. She espouses the law of three: the understanding that whatever we do will be returned to us threefold, that it matters not what we do in this life so long as our actions bring harm to none. She reminds us that all our actions are recorded and, although karma appears patient, it is often ruthless in its delivery. To understand these laws and to live by them with the purest intent, will see us exit this life and journey to the next with a clear memory of our previous life and the lessons learned during that time.

If Crow has flown into your cards today, listen to your instincts and act upon them in a way that honourably serves your purpose. Treat others as you would like to be treated, never expect others to do what you should do yourself and never act in a way that may cause harm to another. Breaking these simple rules will see the strong arm of spiritual law slam down the karmic hammer.

You have all the wisdom and knowledge you need within you to make the right decision. Call upon it now and you cannot make a mistake.

29.
FROG ~ Cleansing

When Frog's chorus is heard, it generally indicates approaching rain. Symbolically, it implies a need to settle the emotional dust that prevents the stream of life from flowing in a productive manner. It promises to cleanse our Spirit by stimulating the release of sacred tears and the freeing of pent up emotion.

Those who live in the Australian Outback look forward to the wet season because it soothes the earth, promising new growth and fertility. In similar fashion, when we welcome our cleansing tears we are reassuring our self that everything will be okay and that all will work out in the end. Instinctively we are preparing our bodies for fruitful new beginnings and the conclusion of emotional barrenness and drought.

When we journey through life denying ourselves of emotional cleansing, we grow numb to the possibility of change. We stop looking for opportunity and signs of new growth. We begin to see life as empty, sterile and deficient and we forget what life was like before the drought. When honoured, though, our tears hold the power to strengthen us and deepen our sense of self-worth. They help us look at life in a bountiful way. Our tears welcome fertility and growth back into our life, but only when they are celebrated. To deny them, or to see them as signs of weakness, is to guarantee a drought that will forever hamper life and any chance of emotional healing. Where there is no love, encouragement or support there is no chance of growth. Without rain, there is no life. Without tears there can be no healing.

If Frog has sung its way into your cards today, you are being encouraged to embrace your tears and to see them as a chance to rid yourself of emotional, physical and spiritual burden. Frog is reminding you to take time out for yourself, to shun negativity and fear and to release emotional baggage.

Frog Dreaming teaches us to welcome and honour our tears and to see them as a healthy way to cleanse the soul of pain, grief, fear and longing. It offers us the chance to recharge our batteries and reclaim a sense of balance and healing in our lives, thus affording us a fertile new ground on which to start again.

30.
BLACK SWAN – Grace

Everyone knows the tale of The Ugly Duckling: a child's fable about an abandoned hatchling forced to endure ridicule and rejection, but who ultimately overcame adversity to become a beautiful Swan. The parable demonstrates that until you can look inside and find the innate beauty that resides there, you cannot expect anybody else to see your beauty. When you look in the mirror and see infinite beauty looking back, however, others will also recognise true beauty (on all levels) when they look at you.

Swan helps us realise our inner beauty by returning us to a state of grace. Grace cannot be learned. It cannot be bought or given – it can only be found within. It must be remembered. Children naturally walk with grace. Grace is innocence and impeccability, coupled with a deep knowing and an unwavering sense of belonging; the knowledge of what true beauty is without having to advertise it.

Without inner beauty, peace and confidence, there is no grace. People who have looked deep within themselves, who have healed their past and reclaimed their inner child, know grace. Grace is the ability to walk through life, head held high with humility, pride and a balanced ego. Grace allows us to be strong, abundant and proud without being aloof, pompous or rude. Grace keeps us grounded and in touch with those less fortunate and those who have not yet reclaimed the knowledge.

If Swan has gracefully floated into your cards today, get ready to recognise your true essence and to trust the grace of your own being. Be prepared to see the golden potential in those around you as you relearn to unconditionally love yourself and radiate the inner beauty that yearns to be discovered. Prepare to awaken the grace that lays dormant. Allow yourself to access Spirit's gifts of self-empowerment so that you may finally learn to believe in yourself on all levels. Ready yourself to transform your sense of abandonment into Mystery so that others may be drawn to you in awe and wonderment instead of being turned away by fear and confusion. Allow your inner beauty to emerge and the world will applaud and shower you with reward. That is Swan's promise to you.

31.
DOLPHIN ~ Breath

Dolphin is one of Spirit's midwives. Dolphin is present when we are born; she helps us take our first breath and then pilots us through life in much the same way as she will guide a boat from port out into the open sea. She reminds us to breathe as we embark on all creative ventures.

The time spent in the womb is sacred. It shapes our view of the world before and after we are born. Realising what life was like for both you and your mother while she was carrying you will help explain why you act and react toward life the way you do, the way you feel toward your family, why you hold your breath in times of stress and why your view of yourself has developed as it has. Your sense of security and confidence, your relationships and even the type of employment you seek, are all influenced by the quality of the time you spent in your mother's womb and the conditions under which you drew your first breath.

You agreed to everything as it is, as it was and as it will be before entering this life. What you do with this understanding and how you let it affect you is the key to a healthy, happy existence.

If the Dolphin has swum into your cards today, you are being prompted to review your life by asking questions that may trigger heartfelt reactions to your time in your mother's womb. Ask yourself what life was like for you and your mother during this time. Consider the possibility that there may be things you are trying to bring to fruition that are unconsciously being blocked by your memory of your time in the womb. Are you symbolically holding your breath as you intuitively remember anxiety, the stress of your mother and your birth, for example? To answer this question, sit in the sacred silence. Still your inner chatter and self-doubt and meditatively journey back through your life to your time in the womb. Relive your birth, your first birthday and every birthday thereafter. They will act as anchors, starting points from which you may proceed to examine your life. Talk to your mother or someone you trust to help you remember. Evaluate the details that stand out and see them as a foundation on which to re-map your journey, to check your life's blueprint and to review the sacred contracts you signed before entering this world. See this as an opportunity to reclaim your power, to rebirth and to finally honour the first breath you ever took.

32.
WHALE - Record Keeper

There are many tales of heroes being swallowed by Whales in their quest for enlightenment. Their descent into the creature's belly often represents mans' spiral into the Underworld and his inevitable re-emergence after certain tests are passed; a journey emblematic of sacred rebirth and retrieval of the human spirit.

Whale asks us to remember the Earth as our Mother and to reconnect with her and the soul connection we forged at the beginning of time. Whale is a keeper of the Earth Mother's sacred records. She witnesses the proceedings that collectively authenticate the spiritual makeup of the Earth; the memories of each and every event that has ever and will ever contribute to her shaping, and stores them within her Dreaming. Whale helps us remember the spiritual history of the areas most significant to our personal journey and offers ways to enhance our medicine, our lives and the planet as a whole.

It is believed that many people who work with Whale hold within their DNA the ability to comprehend the sound frequencies encoded in the audible rhythms and vibrations emitted by the great mammal. The throbbing, metrical song of the Whale offers it the chance to reconnect with universal consciousness and the heartbeat of the Earth Mother, which is reminiscent of the double heartbeat we all heard as we grew in our mothers' wombs.

If the Whale has sung her way into your cards today, the vaults of Creation are being opened to you offering access to the sacred knowledge stored within. Whale is journeying with you, guiding you back to the deep-core rhythms of Nature and your instinctual connection to the cycles of life. She is helping you remember your personal truth and wisdom and how to reconnect to the heartbeat of the Universal Mother.

Whale wants you to rebirth your emotional body and to revive yourself physically by tapping into the knowledge of your own genetic memory and personal rhythm. In doing so you will remember the sacred bond you share with all things and you will ultimately find the knowledge to heal yourself and your family. You may even glean insight into how the rest of humanity could follow suit.

33.
SPIDER – Weaver of Dreams

Spider, as the Weaver of Dreams, reminds us that we are the creators of our own lives and that we alone choose the directions we take.

Every night the Spider weaves her web and every morning she pulls it apart, fully prepared to reweave it later that night. Her web is symbolic of life. We are all essential strands in the Web of Life. Each of us is imbued with strength and wisdom to make a vital contribution to the planet.

Spider encourages us to explore life and to investigate the strands that lead out from the centre of her web. Some will offer reward and others won't. As we journey the positive strands, life seems abundant. A wrong turn though, will present a strand that offers nothing. Life becomes difficult with all attempts to free ourselves proving futile. The Web of Life is riddled with pitfalls, but it also promises greatness to those prepared to take risks and work hard.

As the Weaver of Dreams, Spider urges us to explore life and to reweave our web when our path becomes barren. She helps us reclaim our power and bring our dreams to fruition. She warns, however, that in order to open new doors we must first close old ones by facing our fears and making choices that promise new beginnings.

If Spider has woven her way into your cards today, you are being reminded of your role as a vital strand in the Web of Life. We all yearn to take control of our lives and to make a difference to the world. We all yearn to believe in ourselves, to have faith in our ability to heal and to realise our true potential. Well, you are being reminded that Spider nurtures the wisdom in you to make your healing possible and your life more abundant and fulfilling. Now is the time to acknowledge your vulnerabilities, face your fears and strive to achieve your dreams. So, embrace your Purpose and your Personal Power.

Spider is calling to you to reconnect with Spirit and to remember that you are not apart from the world in which you live, but rather a vital thread in the Universal tapestry. Without your input, the tapestry will fray and eventually fall apart.

INTERPRETING

THE CARDS:

Earth

34.
TURTLE - Mother Earth

Even when surrounded by those we love and respect, we sometimes feel alone and isolated. We sometimes forget our connection to Spirit and the relationship we have with the Earth Mother and Creation. We feel apart from, rather than a part of, nature. We feel disconnected from the Great Wheel of Life and believe ourselves to be alone.

Turtle, however, reminds us that we are never alone – that the Earth is our Mother and that she loves, speaks, protects and provides for us every day.

Due to their ancient heritage, Turtles have long been revered as symbols of the Earth Mother, longevity and protection. Turtle lays her eggs deep within the warm sands of Mother Earth, confiding in her the protection and nurturing of her offspring. She trusts that the Earth Mother will provide them with all they need to develop so that they may emerge as strong, independent representatives of the next generation.

To hide something sacred within the dark abyss of Mother Earth, away from the light of the Grandfather Sun, is symbolic of the ritualistic death endured by individuals of many ancient cultures in their search for healing, ancestral wisdom and spiritual enlightenment.

As the Turtle's young emerge from the sand, they are in fact rebirthing as if from the Womb of the Earth Mother. Their first birth is symbolised by the laying of the egg into the Earth, with the rebirth symbolised by the breaking free of the coffin-like eggshell to emerge from the nurturing energy of Mother Earth into the light of Grandfather Sun.

If Turtle has gently edged her way into your cards today, you are being prepared for profound change - in the form of healing (regarding family issues, secrets, etc.), personal growth and an awakening of sorts. You are literally being prepared for rebirth, emergence and a return to clarity.

You are also being reconnected in a sacred way to the creative force of the Earth Mother's womb, her heart and the inherent wisdom she yearns to impart.

You are being reminded that we are 'all related' and that, even when you believe yourself forsaken; you are being cradled and nurtured by Mother Earth.

35.
TASMANIAN DEVIL –
Purification

The generic name of the Tasmanian Devil, *Sarcophilus*, means 'flesh-lover', indicating its carnivorous dietary preference. Meat is what nourishes the Tasmanian Devil. It instinctively knows that meat is the only fare that will supply it with the strength and endurance to fulfil its duties to Mother Earth.

Choosing the life of the humble yet cantankerous recluse, however, the Tasmanian Devil is a shy creature that prefers to feed on carrion and road kill rather than relying on its skills as a capable hunter. Thus, the Tasmanian Devil is seen as the cleaner, the one whose responsibility it is to ensure that the deceased are returned to Mother Earth as efficiently as possible, minimising the risk of putrefaction and contamination of the land and water ways.

Tasmanian Devil teaches us to purify our lives, to honour our bodies and to exorcise all that is corrupted from our systems. Eating all that is wholesome, drinking all that is pure and honouring our bodies by regularly exercising and getting adequate rest are all lessons afforded by Tasmanian Devil, as is only ever doing what is right for us while avoiding the propensity to base our decisions on what others may do, prefer or expect.

Tasmanian Devils are famous for their powerful jaws and crushing bite. Tasmanian Devil teaches us to honour ourselves on a communication level, therefore, by using the vice-like power of its jaws to speak with vice-like force or, when appropriate, with gentle humility. He validates the art of cutting through pretence to get directly to the heart of the matter, thus purifying our relationships of dishonesty and misunderstanding.

If the Tasmanian Devil has skulked his way into your cards today, you are being prompted to purify some aspect of your life. The cleansing process personified by the appearance of the Tasmanian Devil can be as tender and healing as you like, or equally, as gruesome and devastating. It all depends on how it is approached and whether or not it is handled in a sacred manner.

To remove all that is stagnant from your life is to realise the fertility that comes with release, liberation and freedom. It is to strengthen your foundations and to nourish your desire to expand.

36.
DINGO ~ Trickster

Portrayed as overconfident in many a tale, the simple Dingo artlessly assumes that the world will support his needs, that he will be welcomed and nurtured and that his charm and adaptability will carry him through.

He represents each of us as we naively step out into the world on our own for the first time, ready to begin life. He symbolises the immature character who continually and immediately acts on every impulse, with little consideration of consequence or outcome; an eagerness to venture out into the world, to explore new horizons and to try new things.

Dingo is so keen to step out, however, that he often fails to notice the obstacles that present themselves on a day-to-day basis.

A naturally friendly but socially inexperienced character, Dingo often bites off more than he can chew, then sits licking his wounds in a confused state when his actions inevitably backfire on him.

Although Dingo ostensibly approaches life unaware of the penalties and pitfalls that usually appear painfully obvious to the more mature and street-wise among us, he teaches by example to learn from our mistakes and to never take life too seriously. He espouses that as long as we are able to laugh at ourselves and learn when we trip ourselves up, we will never again fall victim to our own illusory tricks.

If Dingo has blundered his way into your cards today, you may be in need of stabilisation. Perhaps you need to develop a greater sense of responsibility and a more practical, conscientious outlook on life. Are you oblivious to the hazards that are thwarting your true capabilities? Are you fooling yourself that you are precisely on course? Are you overly trusting and a little naïve? Should you rethink things, reassess your current direction and return to your original game-plan?

Like everybody, you have probably made many mistakes; it is now time to learn from them. You cannot expect your life to improve or serve you well when you insist on employing the same strategy with every new venture you embark on.

If you wish to experience new things, try approaching life with a more grounded, practical view instead of being misguided by whim and fancy.

37.
DOG ~ Loyalty

As a demonstration of loyalty in its purest form, Dog embodies unconditional love, faith and tolerance. To treat a Dog with respect and commitment will see it return that love and devotion ten fold, if not more.

Stories abound of Dogs that have dragged their people from burning houses, Dogs that have located lost skiers buried deep under heavy snow or that have travelled great distances against insurmountable odds to return home to their family.

Such is the loyalty of the Dog. It doesn't seem to matter how badly a Dog is treated or neglected, their love remains firm regardless. Or does it?

While Dog strongly believes in loyalty, commitment and hierarchy, she also has faith in maintaining the integrity of our personal values and beliefs. On one hand, for example, she says that before you strive to do anything for yourself, the needs of your pack must first be considered while, on the other, she espouses allegiance to the self first and above all else - particularly when there are young ones involved.

Dog nurtures the ability to forgive when appropriate, to accept imperfection and to maintain truth and loyalty toward others – but more importantly, she demands you treat yourself with the same level of respect. Dog will only take abuse for so long, you see, before she turns on her oppressor in order to regain power, protect herself and retain integrity.

Dog is a powerful teacher that inspires trust, love and acceptance – qualities that can only be harnessed in others when first established in and for the self.

If Dog has loped into your cards today, you are being reminded of the love you have surrounding you at this time; love that you may be taking for granted or that you believe is no longer there. Is your loyalty to another a bit one-sided or no longer nurturing your needs? Are you sacrificing your true feelings for fear of being rejected? Is the loyalty in your relationship out of balance?

Dog Dreaming reminds us to maintain the loyalty we have to ourselves as our prime objective, for without it we cannot expect loyalty or unconditional love to be returned to us in any form.

38.
THYLACINE - Wisdom

A large percentage of Tasmania's wilderness still exists in its virgin state, completely unspoiled by development or land clearing. Many believe, therefore, that the Thylacine endures in secrecy deep within the heart of the Tasmanian forest, protected by both the inaccessibility of its habitat and its elusive nature.

Carrying folklore status on par with the Loch Ness Monster and Yeti, reports of sightings are common, but never substantiated by photographic or videotaped evidence. If the myths are true, and the Thylacine does indeed still subsist, its acumen alone has kept it safe and hidden for almost 70 years.

When life becomes overwhelming, excessively busy or too fast,

Thylacine advocates having the good judgment to withdraw from the mob and walk alone for a spell, perhaps spending time exploring the truths buried deep within the inner landscape.

Thylacine offers a time of calm; the chance to contemplate our purpose and reasoning rather than seeking the counsel of others. She espouses quality time spent in solitude. She prompts us to stop and ask, what is the purpose of my life? Why have I experienced all that I have? Why am I here?

Thylacine represents our desire to seek a deeper reality and a more defined truth. She supports this quest by encouraging us to journey inward to form a relationship with our own thoughts and the natural impulses that instigate our actions.

If Thylacine has crept into your cards today, you are being encouraged to seek out a silent place of solitude. Use this sacred space as a vehicle to better know yourself. Use the sacred silence as a means of deepening your own knowledge and your innate sense of wisdom. Wait until your instincts tell you that the time has come to return to the people, to share your knowledge and hopefully widen the perception of those around you.

Thylacine teaches us to deepen our inherent wisdom, to study it, to become one with it and to share it with others when the time is right.

Gathered over a lifetime of experience, our wisdom is what marks us as unique. It represents the inherent skills we hold that someday may be presented to the world as instruments of healing and learning.

39.
RED KANGAROO - Responsibility

The Red Kangaroo is unique in its ability to maintain three young at once: one at foot, one in the pouch, while a third develops in the womb. As the one at foot is weaned, the one in the pouch exits, making way for the partly formed sibling which instinctively climbs into the pouch directly after birth. With the womb now devoid of life, the female will mate immediately, thus replacing the foetus.

When environmental conditions are fertile and rain is abundant, the feed is lush and plentiful and the weather is benevolent, Red Kangaroos live a productive existence. If the conditions deteriorate however, bringing drought, fire or flood, the female Red Kangaroo will relinquish the infant in her pouch and put the foetus in the womb into a state of suspended animation. The infant remains nourished and is continually fed by the mother, but it does not develop physically. She can sustain the foetus in this way for quite some time, waiting for the conditions of the land to improve so that the Joey can be born into a time of plenty. By surrendering the existence of one Joey and by putting the other into a state of hold, she takes responsibility for her own survival and that of her family.

If Red Kangaroo has leapt into your cards today, you may be feeling as though you have sacrificed a large part of yourself for the benefit of your family. Maybe the time has come to reclaim these aspects instead of harbouring resentment and jealousy.

Are you living in a constant state of stress, for example, barely surviving from one day to the next? If so, do you see this as taking sound responsibility?

If you are a parent, remember that everything you do inherently instils itself in the consciousness of your children as acceptable behaviour. Ask yourself if you are taking your responsibility as parent, partner or principal person seriously.

Are you honouring the pledge of responsibility you made to yourself growing up, or would you say that you were in an emotional drought or dormancy at the moment? If this is the case, it may be time to reanimate some element of yourself, so that you can begin taking responsibility for your life and that of your children in a more productive, abundant manner.

40.
GREY KANGAROO – Abundance

When questioned about what wealth means to you, would you say that having copious amounts of money would definitely seal the deal? If so, it would be a good answer – but the wrong one.

To focus exclusively on the acquisition of money only amplifies how little you have. When you concentrate on your desire to attain money, you are effectively nurturing 'poverty mentality'; a state of mind supported by society and inherited ways of thinking. It feeds poverty mentality because it prevents you from seeing the wealth that surrounds you everyday; the wealth that comes with family and friends.

To know true love is to hold supreme wealth. When you know that wealth rarely takes the form of money or gold, you release the monetary mindset so fear of lack can be transmuted into trust. In doing so, the block obstructing your stream of abundance may be removed forever and greater cash flow will result. Letting go of lack will essentially result in gain.

Grey Kangaroo once offered its rich meat, warm pelt and strong bones, which were useful as cutting and digging implements. Prosperity meant healthy children, a full stomach and a warm, dry sleeping place to the people. They believed the land would provide all they needed and, if they lived in harmony with the Earth Mother, their life would be safe and plentiful as a result. So long as the Grey Kangaroo was there, the people knew they would never know hunger or suffering. Its mere existence promised true abundance.

If Grey Kangaroo has vaulted into your cards today, your life will soon be rich with productive emotion, thought and knowledge. These fundamentals will abundantly serve the personal needs of both you and your family. What you require is currently manifesting and your needs are soon to be met.

Grey Kangaroo reminds us to always separate what we want from what we need, before commencing the hunt for either. To seek what we materialistically want above what we realistically need, will result in continued stagnation.

Grey Kangaroo's appearance acts as a reminder that as children of the Earth, it is our birthright to have all our requirements fulfilled – so long as our requests are offered in a sacred way.

41.
POSSUM ~ Opportunity

Possum inspires us to see opportunity in any condition and to productively harness all opportunities to our best advantage; to gently ride on the back of any circumstantial generosity afforded us until we are comfortably established, after which retreat should be executed in an honourable and discreet manner.

To take opportunity by the horns when it is offered is to believe one hundred percent in your total worth and life purpose. To act on every thought and to honour every possibility as potential for growth is what separates successful people from ordinary folk.

Possum urges us to see our life as a foundation on which great things can be initiated. He encourages us to seek out new experiences and attempt new things. Although the Possum is ideally suited to living in the hollows of trees, the idea of squatting in the roofs of human dwellings poses no moral dilemma for him at all.

If Possum has ambled into your cards today, you are being asked to remember who you are and what agreements you made with yourself before commencing your Earth Walk. What did you want to achieve? Where did you see yourself ultimately?

Pay close attention to the opportunities afforded you at this time, for new ways to develop your abilities and to enhance your growth are on offer right now. Identify and discard all feelings of self-doubt – they simply keep you from furthering your skills and employing your talents to the best of your ability.

Possum's appearance heralds the chance to better yourself and to take your knowledge deeper. Opportunity knocks for those alert to its presence. So long as you are willing to work hard and apply yourself, it is acceptable to gently ride on the back of any opportunity that is presented to you. The wealth locked within the authentic self is filled with great possibility and all it takes is the courage to access it and birth it into the light of day.

Possum's appearance in your cards may also mean that you have a freeloader in your midst – someone who is taking advantage of your generosity. The best way to expel a Possum from your roof is to install a sensor-light. Nocturnal by nature, Possums hate bright light, so with lights turning on at the slightest movement they quickly find an alternate dwelling. Using a similar approach, to illuminate your squatter's sponging ways, visualise their light turning on (and staying on) whenever they enter their bedroom. They will soon find it impossible to stay as a result.

42.
BOWERBIRD – Dowry

The male Bowerbird is famous for its bower – an arbour-like mating nest constructed from interwoven grasses, twigs, bark and rootlets. Looking more like a garden arch than a nest when complete, the bower is decorated with found objects of beauty; odds and ends gathered with passionate intent as decoys to attract and inspire a suitable mate. Satin Bowerbirds for example, have a particular weakness for things coloured blue: blue pen lids, blue drinking straws, pieces of blue paper, blue clothes pegs and blue bottle tops. Any discarded or lost item can make its way into the Satin Bowerbird's nest, so long as it is coloured predominantly in an attractive shade of blue. Expert pilferers, the Bowerbird raids outhouses and potting sheds, searching for its favoured plunder to take back to its bower.

Identifying acquisitiveness as its main weakness, the Bowerbird validates its behaviour by proclaiming it a necessary facet of its Dreaming. It cleverly translates an obviously infatuated mind-set into sensible and realistic preparations for the future. If it were to ignore its innate desire to gather and collect, the male Bowerbird would have nothing to present to its prospective mate as a dowry. From the female Bowerbird's perspective, the male who collects the greatest amount of objects will ultimately prove to be the most suitable mate; the beauty of his bower signifying a superior level of determination, dedication and effort. As with all animals, potential mates are chosen depending on their deservedness and worthiness, with a belief that affirms, 'the stronger the mate, the stronger the offspring', ruling their final decision.

Accumulation and contribution are Bowerbird's gifts to the people.

Prudent observation of what is required while employing appropriate and constructive follow-up action is the message of the Bowerbird. It indicates that when you are readying for change of any sort, the trappings, information and resources required to ensure a successful and abundant future will be available.

By appearing in your cards today, Bowerbird is making preparations for the next phase of your life; encouraging you to begin gathering together all that you need to ensure a productive future for yourself. He is asking you to build your bower; to prepare your dowry, be it in the form of extra or further study, savings, self-worth, spiritual development or something else.

43.
WOMBAT - Gentle Aggression

Equipped with cartilage plating in her rump, a female Wombat will block her burrow by sitting face first just inside the opening when a predator threatens entry. A hungry Dingo, for example, may attempt to force access by chewing on the rump of the Wombat, but with no feeling to weaken its stance the Wombat proves a fearless adversary. Determined to protect her young, she will wait, expecting the Dingo to see the futility in its actions and to wander off. Driven by hunger, the Dingo persists. In this scenario, the Wombat will crouch down, apparently allowing access to the Dingo. Eager to get to the young, the Dingo crawls over the Wombat, wedging itself between the roof of the den and her strong backbone. With the Dingo helplessly stuck, the Wombat stands up, crushing its victim against the roof of the tunnel.

Wombat chooses to express herself assertively first, reverting to aggressive confrontation only when necessary. She relies on the virtue of her rivals, hoping they will see her point. She never wages war as her first plan of attack. She prefers to negotiate initially, expressing herself plainly, regressing to force only when all else fails.

Wombat walks her talk, expressing things exactly as she sees them. She will not be put down or belittled by anyone. She views her opinions, beliefs and values as sacred and definitely worthy of recognition. She insists that others take heed of her opinions and is self-assured enough to outwardly express her demands. If she has to, she will enforce her expectations vehemently, even physically, but until the need arises she expresses herself with influence and tenacity.

If Wombat has moseyed into your cards today, you are being asked to speak with assertiveness instead of irrationally 'hitting the roof' whenever you feel threatened. Wombat allows you to speak up, confronting perceived wrongs with innate confidence and assuredness without being excessively violent or rude.

To treat others as you would like to be treated is the golden rule of the Wombat. She understands how easy it is to feel intolerant toward those who choose to ignore your advice, however, especially when you know it to be wisdom gleaned over a lifetime of experience.

44.
ECHIDNA ~ Personal Protection

When threatened, Echidnas quickly dig themselves into the ground leaving no part visible except for their quills. Such a move precludes anyone from picking them up or altering their path. They effectively shut themselves off from the world, preventing anyone from interfering or getting too close.

Such action not only protects them from predatory attack, but unfortunately also shields them from the assistance or support offered by those who would see no harm come to them. What if the Echidna's quest for food leads him onto a busy road, into oncoming traffic and inevitable danger, for example? What if a passing motorist stops and attempts to direct him off the road? What if the attempts prove futile, because the Echidna's obstinate character prevents him from realising the error of his ways?

Quickly agitated, Echidnas prey on Ants because they know they hold a secret: patience and strength of character. Ant nurtures the collective powers of the mind, body and spirit. It expounds the strength found in community and unity.

If Echidna has shuffled into your cards today, you are being asked to open your heart to the needs of those around you and the nurturing they can offer. Stop shutting people out. You need to let down your guard, relax your sense of personal protection, develop tolerance and begin to trust. Shunning anything (or anyone) that may divert you from your path is great if you want to live an independent life, but Echidna warns against protecting yourself to the point that your heart becomes impenetrable.

Echidna helps us understand the fundamental distinction between denial and determination or, more to the point, the difference between not wanting assistance and not needing support.

The idea of an independent lifestyle may appear attractive - free of the hassles of commitment and responsibility to others, but if you become too complacent you may accidentally find yourself exiled from social activity altogether. Your friends may wander away, for example, and your family may forget to invite you to family events.

To stand rigid and distant from those in your life will eventually give rise to the general belief that you are unapproachable, ungrateful, aggressive and lacking in humility.

Resources:

~~~~~~~~~

- **Cooper, J. C.** *Symbolic and Mythological Animals*. London: Aquarian, 1992.
- **Grey, M.** *Beasts of Albion*. London: Aquarian, 1994
- **King, S. A.** *Animal Dreaming*. Australia: Circle of Stones, 2003
- **King, S. A.** *Animal Messenger*. Australia: New Holland Publishers, 2006
- **Lawlor, R.** *Voices of the First Day: Awakening in the Aboriginal Dreamtime*. Rochester, Vermont: Inner Traditions / Bear and Company, 1991
- **Sams, J. and Carson, D.** *Medicine Cards*. New York: St. Martin's Press, 1988, 1999
- **Walker, B.** *Woman's Dictionary of Myths and Secrets*. NY: Harper Collins, 1983
- **Walker, B.** *Woman's Dictionary of Symbols & Sacred Objects*. London: Pandora, 1988

In praise of 'The Animal Dreaming Oracle Cards'

'Scott's deep reverence and connection with Spirit is obvious. He has created a sincere spiritual card system with an easy approach, ideal for both beginners and experienced readers. Through these cards, animal teachers and the Ancestor Spirits walk with us, interact in our lives and bring their magick into a mundane technical age. They touch the soul, reawaken our connection to Spirit and help us approach life in a way that inspires positive understanding, learning and growth. A joy to read.'

Miranda Gray
www.mirandagray.co.uk
Author of 'Beasts of Albion: using Ancient British Animal Guides for Self-Development' and illustrator of the 'Arthurian Tarot Pack'.

'Finally, an Animal Oracle deck of Miracle proportions! Scott Alexander King's 'Animal Dreaming Oracle' will no doubt inspire the many who are now returning to Mother Earth's symbolic insights for synchronistic answers to life's mystery. Scott's uncanny and innate wisdom about animals, and the healing medicine surrounding their energy, will help all who search for universal truth, understanding and answers beyond logical means. The loving intention and artistic brilliance of these timeless cards make them by far, my favourite Animal Oracle deck.'

Maria Elita
www.mariaelita.com
Author of 'The Miracle'

About the Author:

Scott Alexander King
is a teacher, animal psychic and zoomancer – an individual that examines the habits and appearance of animals to help explain or reveal the future path of other people.

He is also the author of *Animal Dreaming*, a shamanic field guide that offers insight into the wisdom of over 200 indigenous and introduced Australian animals, *Animal Messenger,* which celebrates the medicine of over 340 of the world's most exotic animals, and *Meet your Totem Animal*, a CD that guides its listeners to a place where they inevitably meet their totem or power animal.

Scott and his family are based in the beautiful Yarra Valley, Victoria, Australia, as is his shop, *Circle of Stones*.

To find out about Scott's *Animal Dreaming Workshops*, Animal Spirit Readings and his 3-day Certified Course, visit his website at: **www.animaldreaming.com**

About the Artist:

Karen Branchflower was born in Melbourne, Australia in 1954. She studied Art and Design (Ceramics) and then completed a Diploma of Education before working as a Secondary School Art Teacher for 20 years. Karen has been a resident of the Upper Yarra Valley for nearly 25 years. She now works as a freelance illustrator, painter and sculptor.

Also available from
Blue Angel Gallery, Australia

~~~~~~~~~~~~~~~~~~~~~~~~~~~

'ANIMAL DREAMING' (BOOK)
BY SCOTT ALEXANDER KING

The understanding that animals can be spiritually called upon to assist us in almost every aspect of our lives is a realisation that opens a floodgate of knowledge and power to those who seek their counsel.

Animal Dreaming can be seen as a unique opportunity to broaden one's ability to interpret the symbolic language of the animal kingdom. It brings to the People, possibly for the first time, a comprehensive list of over 200 Australian Animals - introducing them to its readers as totems, teachers, healers and spiritual allies.

Animal Dreaming provides ample guidelines for partaking in your own medicine walk - the ability to 'listen with one's eyes', the chance to discover your own animal totem by means of a guided meditative journey, and how to honour your totem once found. It illustrates quite concisely Australia's seasonal wheel of the year, introduces its readers to what it means to be feral Australian, while expansively listing the spiritual and symbolic interpretations of over 200 native, domesticated and introduced animals, birds, insects, reptiles and fish.

Animal Dreaming is an Australian first and a must have for anyone interested in Earth Wisdom and rudimentary Shamanic Lore.

"Animal Dreaming is a powerful, comprehensive and accessible handbook on how to tap into the wisdom of animal spirit guides. Mr. King has done a remarkable job of detailing the spiritual characteristics of both feral and indigenous animals of Australia. For those on the spiritual path, you'll find this book useful for many years to come."
Dr. Steven Framer
Author of *Sacred Cermonies: How to Create Ceremonies for Healing, Transitions and Celebrations*

'ASK AN ANGEL'
ORACLE CARD SET
BY TONI CARMINE SALERNO & CARISA MELLADO

Ever wished you could ask the angels questions
and get clear answers in response?
Well now, using the "Ask An Angel" cards and guidebook, you can!

This inspirational card set, featuring the illuminating artwork of best-selling artist and author Toni Carmine Salerno, allows you to quickly and easily receive answers to your questions and gain deeper insight into your current state of being.

The set comprises 42 cards encased in a tarot pouch and a 124-page guidebook, complete with an 'Angel Dictionary,' which provides a greater understanding of the angels and their current and historical roles and associations. Also including a section on 'Communicating with the Angels,' the 'Ask An Angel' cards are a set you will treasure.

The detailed information on how to use the cards and the various card-spreads contained in the guidebook will enable you to give in-depth readings for yourself and others, allowing the loving guidance and support of the angelic realm to be a constant and powerful healing presence in your life.

'CRYSTAL ORACLE'
ORACLE CARD SET
BY TONI CARMINE SALERNO

This beautifully presented set of guidance cards featuring crystals, gems and minerals with an easy-to-use guidebook is designed to inspire and heal you as you connect to the profound love and wisdom which stems from the heart of the Earth.

The accompanying guidebook also includes various card spreads, so you can always get the answers you are seeking.

Features 44 cards & guidebook, packaged in a hard-cover box set.

~~~~~~~~~~~~~~~~~~~~~~~~~~~~~~~~~~~

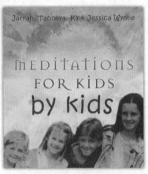

'MEDITATIONS FOR KIDS BY KIDS' (BOOK)
BY JARRAH, TAHNAYA, KY & JESSICA WYNNE

In this touching collection of meditations, the Wynne children - Jessi (age 11), Ky (age 9), Tahnaya (age 7) and Jarrah (age 4) - have created a book to uplift, inspire and nurture kids of all ages!

"These words and pictures will take children away from the rush, bustle and harsh realities of the world, opening up a world full of imagination that is endless, safe and full of love. It will encourage them to connect with their feelings, release their fears and worries and provide them with some coping strategies in these days where beauty and innocence are so often forgotten."
Helen Schweiger - Pre-school Teacher

'THE PHILOSOPHERS' SECRET FIRE:
A HISTORY OF THE IMAGINATION' (BOOK)
BY PATRICK HARPUR

Is there any place for the ancient myths of our ancestors in modern times? Could their shadowy presence in our common imagination be more influential than we realize?

Across the globe many societies still believe in an Otherworld of spirits, gods and daimons, which the West has banished to the unconscious mind and now only visits in dreams. Yet this visionary tradition continues to subvert the rational universe, erupting out of the shadows in times of intense religious and philosophical transition. In his dazzling history of the imagination, Patrick Harpur links together fields as far apart as Greek philosophy and depth psychology, Renaissance magic and tribal ritual, Romantic poetry and the ecstasy of the shaman, to trace how myths have been used to make sense of the world. He uncovers that tradition which alchemists imagined as a Golden Chain of initiates, who passed their mysterious 'secret fire' down through the ages. As this inspiring book shows, the secret of this perennial wisdom is of an imaginative insight: a simple way of seeing that re-enchants our existence and restores us to our own true selves.

"Harpur leads us through history's secret chambers with such grace of language and insight that we forget the hour. In each chapter, Harpur expertly cuts a new facet of the philosophers' stone, adding plane upon plane until the light breaks open vast multidimensional realities beyond our imagination. I would make Harpur's book required reading for every student of philosophy, depth psychology and history"
Dianne Skafte, author of *When Oracles Speak*

"A sublime read."
The Guardian

"It would be hard to overestimate the value of Harpur's book or to praise it too highly. We're offered a timely reminder to recall our larger mystical selves, to conceive of possibilities of transformation, to remove the constraints from our limited notion of reality and celebrate life's infinite and sacred inventiveness."
Rosie Jackson, author of *The Eye of the Buddha*

For more information
or to purchase any
Blue Angel Gallery release,
please visit our website at:

www.blueangelonline.com